21ˢᵗ Century Skills Library

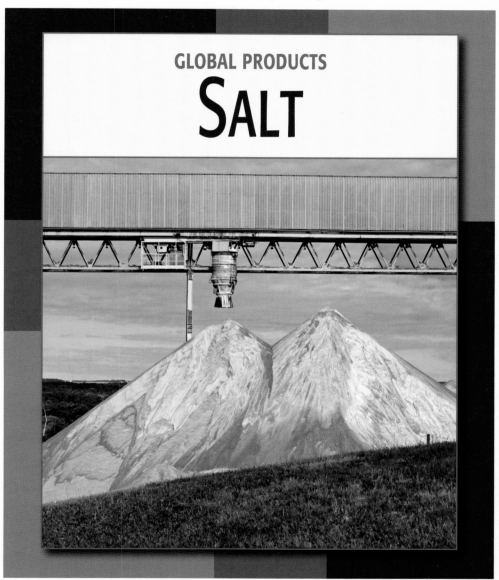

GLOBAL PRODUCTS

SALT

Nancy Robinson Masters

Cherry Lake Publishing
Ann Arbor, Michigan

CHERRY LAKE Publishing

Published in the United States of America by Cherry Lake Publishing
Ann Arbor, Michigan
www.cherrylakepublishing.com

Content Adviser: Dennis S. Kostick, Senior Mineral Commodity Specialist, U.S. Geological Survey, Reston, Virginia

Photo Credits: Cover and page 1, © Bronwyn Photo, used under license from Shutterstock, Inc.; page 4, Courtesy of Dennis S. Kostick, U.S. Geological Survey; page 7, Courtesy of Kansas Underground Salt Museum; page 8, © Andrew Woodley/Alamy; page 11, © POPPERFOTO/Alamy; page 12, Courtesy of Kansas Underground Salt Museum; page 14, © Mark Boulton/Alamy; page 17, ©Helene Rogers/Alamy; page 19, © Grzegorz Slemp, used under license from Shutterstock, Inc.; page 20, © Jeff Greenberg/ Alamy; page 21, Courtesy of Kansas Underground Salt Museum; page 23, © puchan, used under license from Shutterstock, Inc.; page 25, © Juniors Bildarchiv/Alamy; page 27, © Florida Images/Alamy

Map by XNR Productions Inc.

Library of Congress Cataloging-in-Publication Data
Masters, Nancy Robinson.
  Salt / by Nancy Robinson Masters.
    p. cm.—(Global products)
  Includes index.
  ISBN-13: 978-1-60279-120-6
  ISBN-10: 1-60279-120-1
  1. Salt—Juvenile literature. I. Title. II. Series.
TN900.M27 2008
553.6'32—dc22   2007038843

*Cherry Lake Publishing would like to acknowledge the work of
The Partnership for 21st Century Skills.
Please visit* www.21stcenturyskills.org *for more information.*

TABLE OF CONTENTS

CHAPTER ONE

THERE'S MORE TO SALT THAN MEETS THE FRIES

Cube-shaped salt crystals are used to make thousands of items, including the salt that flavors our food.

Alice Abernathy licked the last grains of salt from her fingers. She took a drink from her water bottle and handed the sack of French fries to Jimmy Nevan, who was sitting beside her in the backseat of the van.

"Look at it snow! Those cows look really, really cold out there!" She said, pressing her nose against the window.

She was glad Jimmy's parents had invited her to make the trip to Hutchinson, Kansas, with them. She had never been to Kansas before. Jimmy and his family lived in Koolyanobbing, a town in Western Australia. They were staying with Alice's family in Missouri while visiting the United States.

"Thanks, cobber," Jimmy said to her as he pulled a fry from the sack. "These are the best chips I've had since I left Australia. Good thing this road isn't iced over or we might have a bingle."

"Okay, Jimmy. I know 'cobber' means friend, and 'chips' are what you Aussies call French fries. But what's a bingle?"

"A bingle is a minor car crash," he explained as the van's tires suddenly squished to a stop in slush covering the parking lot of the Hutchinson Salt Company. "No worries. We're right on time."

"Right on time for what?"

"Right on time for the Dark Ride through the Kansas Underground Salt Museum!" he exclaimed. "Follow me!"

Salt occurs naturally in many parts of the world, both above and below the earth's surface. Almost all of the water on Earth—97 percent—contains salt. The chemical name for the most common form of salt is **sodium chloride**. The molecules that make up salt form cube-shaped crystals.

Did you know that salt is the only rock humans eat? But salt is not just for preparing or seasoning food. Out of every 10 spoonfuls of salt produced, only one-quarter of a spoonful of salt ends up in a saltshaker or fast-food packet. The other nine and three-quarters spoonfuls will be used in more than 14,000 other ways.

Most of the world's salt is used as a raw material by chemical industries. The products made with these raw materials are all around us, but we don't recognize them as being made with salt. Salt not only flavors French fries, it is also used to make the paper sacks French fries come in, windows, feed for cows, and tires.

Salt even produces slush in parking lots. Almost one-third of the salt produced in the United States is used to keep highways and other paved surfaces free of ice in freezing weather.

CHAPTER TWO

PLEASE PASS THE SALT!

*People wear hard hats and casrry flashlights when they
step off the elevator that takes them to the entrance
of the Kansas Underground Salt Museum.*

"**G**ood-oh!" Jimmy cheered as he stepped off the double-decker

elevator that carries visitors 650 feet (198 m) below the ground to the

Kansas Underground Salt Museum entrance. "We don't have to go

Workers use small boats to harvest salt in Senegal.

underground to find salt in Koolyanobbing. My dad is a salt jackaroo. He harvests salt right off the surfaces of lakes where it collects."

"What's a salt jackaroo?" Alice asked as they waited for their turn to ride in the museum tour **tram**.

"I'll explain later. Hold on to your hard hat and flashlight when you climb into the tram! Off we go!"

As early as 2200 B.C., salt was produced **commercially** in China by boiling **brine** in clay pots to make dried salt cakes. The dried salt cakes were traded for other items. As the demand for salt increased, salt merchants pressed salt into the shape of small coins. Explorer Marco Polo discovered that these salt coins were valued as much as metals such as silver and gold in Asia in the 11th century. At about the same time, in West Africa on the edge of the Sahara desert, an ounce of salt could be traded for an ounce of gold. Salt is still used for trade among **nomads** in some places in Africa today.

The human body cannot produce salt, but it needs salt in order to function properly. A book published in China about 4,700 years ago described more than 40 different ways salt could be used for medical treatments. Many people still use some of these treatments, like gargling with salt water to help ease a sore throat.

In the ancient world, salt was not only necessary for life, but also for death. Dry salt and natron, a

21st Century Content

One of the goals of the United Nations Children's Fund (UNICEF) is for every child in the world to use salt that contains **iodine**, known as iodized salt. This is because the human body needs a very small amount of iodine to stay healthy.

Chile is the world's top producer of iodine because of the iodine-rich soil found there. Japan is second. The United States is third. People in countries with soil that does not contain enough iodine, such as Laos, can be severely affected by iodine deficiency. The Laotian government passed a law in 1993 that all salt sold in Laos must have iodine added. As a result, the health of the Laotian people is improving dramatically.

mixture of various sodium compounds, were used to preserve the bodies of dead people. Although Egyptian mummies are the most well-known, mummies preserved with salt have been found in other places throughout the world.

Wars were often won or lost, depending on which army had adequate salt for eating, preserving meat, fighting diseases, and treating wounds. During the American Revolution (1775–1783), the British tried to cut off all salt supplies to General George Washington's army. In the winter of 1812, thousands of soldiers in Napoleon's army died from wounds that would not heal due to a lack of salt. Some of the fiercest battles in the American Civil War (1861–1865) were fought for control of salt sources.

Chinese emperor Hsia Yu collected the first **tax** on salt about 6,000 years ago. Pirates became rich capturing ships carrying salt. Smuggling salt to avoid paying taxes was a serious crime in England in 1765. A salt tax was one of the reasons for the French Revolution in 1789.

In 1930, Mahatma Gandhi marched 248 miles (399 km) to get salt from the ocean rather than pay the high tax the British government placed on salt in India. Gandhi's salt tax protest made him famous and led to India gaining independence from British rule.

Not everyone opposed paying salt taxes. Salt producers in the United States voluntarily paid a salt tax to help build the Erie Canal. This inland waterway connected the Great Lakes with the Hudson River and made it cheaper and faster to move heavy shipments of salt to customers. The Erie Canal opened in 1825 and is still known as "the ditch that salt built."

The total amount of salt produced in the world in 2006 was 240 million metric tons. That would fill more than 529 billion 1-pound (454 gram)

Mahatma Gandhi led a march to the sea in 1930 to protest the high tax on salt in India.

boxes of salt! The United States was the world's leading producer of salt until 2006. That year, China produced more salt than any other country. China is expected to continue to be the leader in global salt production in the 21st century.

CHAPTER THREE

HARVESTING THE SALT OF THE EARTH

Miners use dynamite to blast through huge layers of rock salt like these layers in the Kansas Underground Salt Museum.

"What a blast!" Alice squealed as the tram came to a stop. "Viewing those salt displays made me really, really thirsty. I can't believe that the temperature is always 68 degrees down here no matter how hot or cold it is outside. And I can't believe that we are 65 stories below the ground!"

Jimmy agreed. "I can hardly wait to tell my mates in Australia how salt is harvested from an underground mine in Kansas."

"You still haven't told me what a salt jackaroo is," Alice reminded him.

"A jackaroo is a man who works at a sheep station. That's like a farm in the United States. My dad drives a grading machine at the salt farm. He rounds up salt like a sheepherder rounds up sheep. So that makes him a salt jackaroo."

"So, if I worked at a salt farm, I would be a salt jillaroo!"

"Good on you!" he laughed. "Now let's go round up a drink of water."

Salt is used in thousands of manufacturing processes. You may already know that it is used to make many food products, such as ketchup, pepperoni, and sports drinks. But did you know that is it also used to make basketballs, computers, and lunch trays?

Before salt can be used to make a product, it has to be obtained by commercial salt producers. There are three ways salt is produced.

The first way is the natural evaporation of salt water by the sun and wind, which produces solar salt. Salt water is captured in lakes, naturally formed shallow ponds, or ponds created especially for solar evaporation. It can take from one to five years to produce a crop of solar salt.

Solar evaporation is the salt production method used by the W. A. Salt Supply operation in Koolyanobbing, Australia. When the water

Sea salt is harvested from these fields in France. The shallow water evaporates and leaves salt behind.

in its salt lake evaporates, workers harvest the salt that is left behind. They use machines to scrape the salt up into rows. A machine picks up this salt, loads it into trucks, and takes it to the washing plant.

After the salt is washed, it is stored for later use or transported by train to a nearby seaport. Each salt car on a train can hold 46,305 pounds

(21,004 kilograms) of salt. Ships along Australia's western coast carry salt packaged in 55-pound (25 kg) bags to 2,205-pound (1,000 kg) bulk containers to customers around the world.

The second way salt is produced is by mining dry salt from underground salt deposits. Tall columns of salt deposits can be anywhere from 500 feet (152.4 m) to more than 2,000 feet (609.6 m) below Earth's surface. Miners use a tool called an undercutter to make deep cuts into the bottom of the column. Small holes are drilled horizontally into the face of the salt and then packed with explosives. When there are no people in the mine, the explosives are set off. Tons of rock salt are blasted off the walls. These chunks are crushed in machines, sorted by size into containers, and hauled up to the surface for more sorting.

Most rock salt from underground mines is used to maintain winter road and highway safety. The salt is treated with a chemical to prevent

Learning & Innovation Skills

Some salt lakes are called terminal lakes. That is because the water flowing into the lake has no way to flow back out, so it cannot leave. Some of the largest terminal lakes in the world include the Caspian Sea north of Iran, the Aral Sea in Uzbekistan, Lake Balkhash in Kazakhstan, and the Great Salt Lake in the state of Utah in the United States.

Pollution of terminal lakes and dams built to divert water from them can cause problems for some animals. For example, the Great Salt Lake provides **brine shrimp** to millions of resident and migratory birds. But pollution and lower water levels can affect the brine shrimp population. What do you think will happen if terminal salt lakes are not protected from pollution and preserved in the 21st century?

it from clumping. Then it is transported by ship, truck, or rail to customers.

The third way salt is produced is solution mining. Vertical wells are drilled into an underground salt deposit. Then water is pumped down to dissolve the salt. This makes brine. Most of the brine is used to make chemicals. Some is used to make vacuum pan salt. To make vacuum pan salt, the brine is pumped up and piped to enclosed evaporation containers, where it is boiled. The salt left in the containers after the water in the brine is boiled away is the purest of all salts. It is the salt you usually find in your saltshaker.

Small amounts of salt are also produced through desalination of salt water. Desalination forces salt water through a special filter that separates the salt from the water. Some of this salt is refined for use. Most, however, is pumped back into the ocean, sea, or into underground storage wells. There are about 7,500 desalination plants in the world.

Salt is removed from seawater at this desalination plant in Abu Dhabi, United Arab Emirates.

Let's take a look at how salt is used to make one product—pickles. Salt is an essential ingredient for making pickles, a food that is produced and eaten in some form in almost every country in the world. More than 5 million pounds (2.27 million kg) of pickles are eaten each day.

Pickles begin as cucumbers. Farmworkers harvest them by hand or with machines. The cucumbers are carried in baskets or transported by trucks to the producer's processing area.

Sorting, inspecting, and washing the cucumbers is the first step in the pickle-making process. Next, the cucumbers are transferred to large, airtight containers that are filled with brine made of water and salt. They are stored in these containers for about five weeks. In large commercial operations, these containers can hold more than 40,000 pounds (18,144 kg) of cucumbers!

The third step is draining the salt water from the cucumbers. Then the cucumbers are washed with fresh water. They are cut into slices, chips, or other shapes and packed into jars. The jars are then filled with liquid made of vinegar, salt, and spices that produce either sweet, sour, or dill pickles.

In the fourth step, the jars are capped and moved to the pasteurization process. Cucumbers can spoil during the brine and packing process if they are exposed to air for too long. Pasteurization heats the jars of pickles and juice to kill bacteria.

Pickles are vacuum-packed in the fifth step. The air is removed from the jar before it is sealed. That's why you hear a "pop" when the jar is opened.

Finally, a label is attached to the jar. The jars are ready to be packed and shipped to local stores or **exported** to other countries.

Pickles made in the United States are exported to 35 countries, including Canada, Mexico, Japan, South Korea, and the Netherlands. The United States also **imports** ready-to-eat pickles and bulk-brined pickles

Cucumbers are soaked in a brine of water and salt to make pickles.

*Pickles come in many different varieties and
all of them are made with salt.*

(cucumbers that are packed in salt water and need further processing before they are sold) from India, Canada, Mexico, Turkey, Honduras, Sri Lanka, Israel, and other countries.

A small cucumber that is grown and harvested in India may be packed in brine made with salt from Poland, shipped to the United States, processed into a sweet pickle, and packed in a jar that is labeled and then shipped to pickle customers in South Korea. No matter where they are made or sold, there would be no pickles in the world without salt.

CHAPTER FOUR

ROADBLOCKS TO SALT

"**H**oly smokes! It's Batman!" Jimmy could hardly believe what he saw. Displayed in the underground gallery next door to the gift shop were the actual costumes and props from several of his favorite movies!

"Is this what happens to all movie costumes and props?" Alice asked the gift shop clerk.

"Not all of them, but some," the clerk explained.

The costume worn by George Clooney in the movie Batman Returns *is on display in the Kansas Underground Salt Museum.*

The Wieliczka Salt Mine in Poland has been in existence for hundreds of years. Through the centuries, some of the miners who worked there used their spare time to create works of art carved from the salt. The mine has been named a World Heritage Site. Tourists can walk through part of the mine to learn more about the history of salt mining and to view the incredible works of art made entirely of salt.

Three miners demonstrated their creativity and **persistence** by sculpting what is known as the Underground Cathedral. The cathedral's altar, religious statues, and even its chandeliers are made of salt. How persistent were the miners? They spent 68 years creating their masterpiece!

"There are millions of other items from all over the world stored in the underground storage vaults built here after the salt was mined. Original sound recordings, cartoons, and movie films like *The Wizard of Oz* are safe here. Not even a Kansas tornado can reach them. This salt mine is the largest international storage facility for movie and television film on Earth."

"Or under it!" Jimmy added.

Access to salt and salt products is convenient in Kansas. In fact, salt deposits are found beneath many states in the United States, and salt is produced in more than 100 other countries. Three main barriers limit access to salt and salt products in other countries.

First, natural barriers to salt occur in countries like Japan, where the land does not contain sodium chloride. Natural barriers also occur in countries that do not have access to oceans, seas, or inland salt lakes.

Miners carved many sculptures out of salt in the Wieliczka Salt Mine.

Second, cultural barriers can also limit access to salt and salt products. In the country of Nepal, for example, fine grain salt imported from neighboring India is iodized before it is sold in the marketplaces. The

Companies that sell a product, such as salt, can make more money if that product can be used in different ways. Through the years, salt producers have developed forms of salt that can be used in many industries.

Which of the forms of salt listed below is used to make bubble bath? To bake pastries? To inject medicine? Feed minerals to cattle? Prepare food? Clean swimming pools?

> Fine grains
>
> Large granules
>
> Flakes
>
> Tablets
>
> Blocks
>
> Liquid

Fine grains of salt are used for baking pastries. Large granules are used for making bubble bath. Flakes are used for food preparation. Tablets are used for cleaning swimming pools. Blocks are used for feeding minerals to cattle. And liquid is used to inject medicine. If these were your answers, you are salt smart!

Nepalese people have used large crystal salt for many centuries. Many of them do not want to use iodized salt from India because it is not the kind of salt that they have traditionally used.

Third, modern trade barriers sometimes limit access to salt and salt products. The World Trade Organization (WTO) and the Salt Institute work to help countries overcome these trade barriers. The WTO is an international organization that establishes rules that affect global trade. It works to improve trade between salt-producing countries and countries with no salt production.

CHAPTER FIVE

SALT IN YOUR FUTURE

Blocks of salt are used to feed minerals to cows and other livestock.

"**O**oroo, cobber," Jimmy said as he put his suitcase in the van.

"Good-bye to you, too," Alice answered. "Thanks again for letting me go with you to Kansas last week. Don't forget your jar of pickles! I hope you don't eat all of them before you get home to Koolyanobbing."

"Right-oh! That jar of pickles is my second-favorite trip souvenir. Making friends with you is my first!"

Zout is the Dutch word for salt. In France, it is *sel.* If you order salt in Spain, ask for *sal,* but in Turkey ask for *tuz.* If you want to buy salt in a market in Indonesia, ask for *garam.* No matter what language you use to say it, salt is a global product almost everyone on Earth recognizes.

Researchers are working with salt to produce amazing new products. For example, a battery made of paper no larger than a candy wrapper is being developed. It will use salt from your body to power handheld electronics.

New technology is also being developed to measure the amount of salt in the air, soil, and water. This will help environmental workers monitor salt levels and reduce the impact of salt on these natural resources. This is important in places such as Chicago, Illinois. The city is covered in salt dust during the winter because of the 140,000 tons of de-icing salt used to keep its roads safe.

Some of the most exciting salt discoveries of the 21st century may come from out of this world. *Opportunity,* the name of the National Aeronautics and Space Administration's Mars rover, has gathered rocks

Trucks with salt spreaders put salt on roads to melt ice during winter storms.

believed to contain ordinary salt on Mars. Maybe some of the salt in the shakers of the future will come from another planet in our solar system!

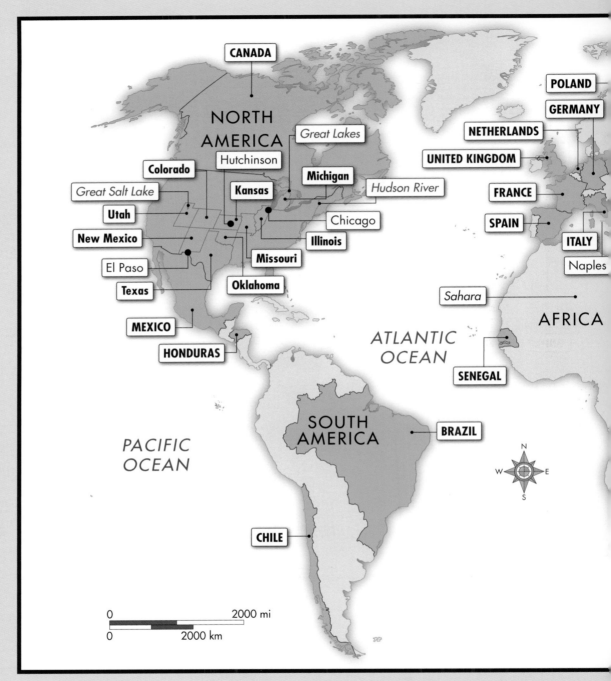

This map shows the countries and cities mentioned in the text.

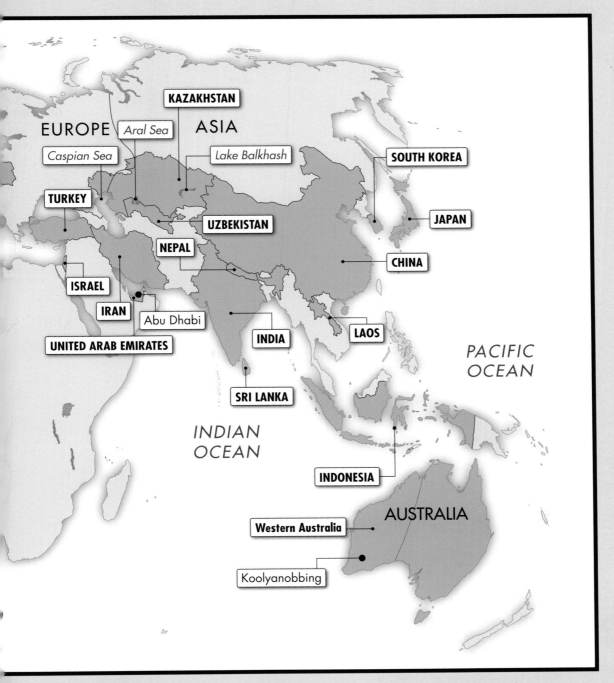

EUROPE

ASIA

KAZAKHSTAN

Aral Sea

Caspian Sea

Lake Balkhash

SOUTH KOREA

TURKEY

JAPAN

UZBEKISTAN

NEPAL

CHINA

ISRAEL

IRAN

Abu Dhabi

UNITED ARAB EMIRATES

INDIA

LAOS

PACIFIC
OCEAN

SRI LANKA

INDIAN
OCEAN

INDONESIA

AUSTRALIA

Western Australia

Koolyanobbing

They are the locations of some of the companies involved in producing and selling salt.

GLOSSARY

brine (BRINE) very salty water

brine shrimp (BRINE SHRIMP) small crustaceans that can live in very salty water

commercially (kuh-MUR-shuhl-ee) having to do with the buying and selling of things

exported (eks-PORT-ed) shipped (such as items) to another country for sale

halite (HAH-lite) rock salt

imports (IM-ports) to bring items in from another country

iodine (EYE-uh-dine) a chemical element that is found in soil, seaweed, and salt water

nomads (NO-madz) people who move from place to place instead of living permanently in one location

persistence (pur-SIS-tuns) the quality of being able to continue for a long time, and work through problems or obstacles to completing a task

polyvinyl chloride (pah-lee-vi-nul KLOR-ide) a chemical compound used in making electronics, pipes, and other products

sodium chloride (SO-dee-um KLOR-ide) a chemical compound made of equal numbers of sodium and chlorine atoms; salt

tax (TAKS) money that people and businesses pay to the government

textile (TEK-stile) woven or knitted fabric or cloth

tram (TRAM) a cart that runs on rails used by miners

FOR MORE INFORMATION

Books

Kurlansky, Mark, and S. D. Schindler (illustrator). *The Story of Salt*. New York: G. P. Putnam, 2006.

Miller, Ron. *The Elements*. Minneapolis: Twenty-First Century Books, 2006.

Web Sites

Cargill Salt—Kids' Page
www.cargill.com/sf_bay/kidspage.htm
Interesting facts about salt and salt experiments to try at home or school

Kidipede—History for Kids: Salt
www.historyforkids.org/learn/food/salt.htm
Find out more about the history of salt

Salt Institute
www.saltinstitute.org
Learn more about the salt industry and the many uses for salt

USGS Minerals Information—Salt
minerals.usgs.gov/minerals/pubs/commodity/salt
Facts about salt and links to more information

INDEX

ABOUT THE AUTHOR

Nancy Robinson Masters loves anything salty! She is an award-winning author, speaker, and licensed airplane pilot who explores the world in search of stories to share with readers of all ages. She is the author of hundred of articles and stories as well as numerous books, including *Jeans* and *Airplanes*, two other titles in the Global Products series. Nancy and her husband, Bill, live on a farm near Abilene, Texas, with their two dogs, four cats, and a pantry full of pickles!